LIGHTHOUSES

LIGHTHOUSES

COURAGE
BOOKS

AN IMPRINT OF RUNNING PRESS
PHILADELPHIA • LONDON

FRONT COVER PHOTO: Heceta Head Light, near Florence, Oregon, USA
  by © Kathleen Norris Cook
BACK COVER PHOTO: Portland Head Light. Cape Elizabeth, Maine, USA
  by © Ron Dahlquist/SuperStock
BACK FLAP: Heceta Head Light, near Florence, Oregon, USA
  by © Gary Benson/Stone/Getty Images

Printed in China

9   8   7   6   5   4   3   2   1
Digit on the right indicates the number of this printing.

ISBN-13: 978-0-7624-2640-9
ISBN-10: 0-7624-2640-3
Library of Congress Control Number: 2005903190

Designed by Amanda Richmond and Susan Van Horn
Edited by Michael Tomolonis
Introduction by Heather Henson
Photos researched by Susan Oyama

This book may be ordered by mail from the publisher.
But try your bookstore first!

Published by Courage Books, an imprint of
Running Press Book Publishers
125 South Twenty-second Street
Philadelphia, Pennsylvania 19103-4399

Visit us on the web!
www.runningpress.com

TABLE OF CONTENTS

INTRODUCTION

Lighthouse on the Island of Pharos.
Alexandria, Egypt. Woodcut, 19th century.

Since the beginning of time, men and women have been drawn to the sea—for adventure, for profit, for a chance to begin life anew on some distant shore. And for as long as there have been voyagers on the rivers, lakes, and oceans of the world, there have been beacons to help guide them to safety.

Thousands of years ago, Greeks, Romans, Egyptians, and Phoenicians lit bonfires on hilltops and cliffs to help guide their sailors along treacherous shores. The earliest references to such beacons are found in Homer's *Iliad*, and *Odyssey*, both written in the 8th century B.C.

As time passed, people began to realize that elevated fires could be seen from a greater distance and so they began to build wood or stone towers with tended fires burning at the top. Around 280 B.C., the Egyptians built the first great lighthouse of history, the Pharos of Alexandria.

The Pharos stood 450 feet tall—at the time the tallest structure in the world. For centuries it guided ships to the world's busiest seaport, and even today, it lives on in the language of the sea. In France, the word for lighthouse is *phare;* in Spain and Italy, *faro.* In English, the study of lighthouse technology is "pharology."

The Romans were next. As they began to expand their vast empire, they built a system of lighthouses along the coasts of Asia, Africa, and Europe. Ruins of their well-built structures can still be seen today on the shores of France and Great Britain. The Phoenicians, a great seafaring people, sailed to distant lands as well, establishing a trading route marked by beacons to safeguard their ships filled with precious cargo.

Lighthouse construction slowed during the Dark Ages, when there was a sharp decline in travel and trade. But by 1100, Italy and France were taking the lead in lighthouse design and construction, and Great Britain was following suit, establishing beacons along its coasts and dotting its colonies with light. By 1716, Boston Light—America's first lighthouse—was built by the Massachusetts Bay colonists at the entrance to Boston Harbor.

The nineteenth and twentieth centuries saw huge advances in lighthouse design and engineering. But slowly, modern technology began to eclipse the need for visual navigational aides. Today's ships navigate using radar and satellites and other invisible, powerful signals. More and more, lighthouses are being transformed into museums and parks—shining beacons to the world's past.

Throughout history, lighthouses have held a special place in our hearts and minds. They are mysterious yet comforting structures. They are symbols of adventure and despair, monuments to humanity's innate wanderlust and to our helplessness in the face of nature.

LIGHTHOUSES THROUGH HISTORY

Around 280 B.C. Ptolemy II, king of Egypt, commissioned the architect Sostratus to design a beacon which "shall serve every man who voyages in a boat." The elaborate three-story marble tower took thousands of slaves twenty years to build. When the Pharos of Alexandria was completed, it was deemed one of the Seven Wonders of the World.

The light burning at the top of the Pharos could be seen from a distance of thirty miles—a miraculous feat at that time.

The great Pharos remained standing for nearly 1600 years—longer than any lighthouse in history. No one knows exactly what happened, but in 1349 the lighthouse was found in ruins, probably the result of an earthquake.

Lighthouse
Sylt Island
Germany

The Pyramids first, which in Egypt were laid;

Next Babylon's Garden, for Amytis made,

Then Mausolos' Tomb of affection and guilt;

Fourth, the temple of Dian in Ephesus built;

The Colossus of Rhodes, cast in brass to the sun;

Sixth, Jupiter's Statue, by Phidias done;

The Pharos of Egypt comes last, we are told,

Or the Palace of Cyrus, cemented with gold.

Seven Wonders of the World, Anonymous

LEGEND TELLS US THAT THE COLOSSUS OF RHODES WAS BUILT BY THE GREEKS NOT LONG AFTER THE PHAROS WAS COMPLETED. THE COLOSSUS WAS SUPPOSEDLY A GIGANTIC, TEN-STORY-HIGH BRONZE STATUE OF A MAN STRADDLING THE ENTRANCE TO THE HARBOR OF RHODES. ALTHOUGH NOT A LIGHTHOUSE PER SE, THE FIGURE HELD A LANTERN HIGH ABOVE HIS HEAD, GUIDING SHIPS TO SAFE PORT.

Strombolicchio Lighthouse
Aeolian Islands
Italy

La Tour d'Orde, also known as Caligula's Light, was built in Boulogne, France by order of the notorious Roman Emperor Caligula. In 40 A.D., it rose 192 feet above a cliff overlooking the English Channel. When Henry VIII captured Boulogne in 1544, La Tour d'Orde was converted into a fort.

The Phoenicians built the **Tower of Hercules** about 100 A.D. on the coast of Spain. It is the only ancient lighthouse which was still in use during the 20th century.

Phare du Ploumanach
Island of Bréhat, Brittany Coast
France

The first great lighthouses were built on land, where it was easy to transport supplies and labor. These early beacons did little to protect ships from the dangerous rocks and reefs lying miles offshore.

France was the first to build a lighthouse in the middle of the vast, wind-tossed sea. It took twenty-seven years, but

La Tour de Cordouan,

an extravagant structure built on a tiny strip of sand five miles off the coast of France in 1622, proved that lighthouses could be built almost anywhere.

Na Popis Lighthouse
Sa Dragonera Island, Balearic Islands
Spain

The next astonishing beacon of history was the Eddystone Light, built near a terrifying stretch of jagged rocks and deadly currents in the English Channel. Often referred to as "the most famous lighthouse in the world," the Eddystone was actually a series of four lighthouses which took a total of two hundred years to build.

The first Eddystone Lighthouse was built in 1695 by Henry Winstanley, an inventor, jokester, and magician. A fanciful structure with balconies, flagpoles, and ornamental gadgets, it was washed away in a storm three years after it was completed—along with its eccentric builder.

John Rudyerd designed the second Eddystone Light as a round, smooth tower so that waves could easily wash over it—a design which became the model for all future lighthouses. Rudyerd had the right idea, but the wrong material: wood. Twenty-five years after it was completed, a fire destroyed the tower.

Wood was not a good choice for building material. Not only were towers built from wood at risk from fire, they also rotted from saltwater and were prone to sea worms which acted like termites, destroying a structure from within.

The third Eddystone Light was built by engineer John Smeaton in 1759. Using Rudyerd's round design, Smeaton invented a new system of dovetailed granite blocks. The structure was fireproof and solid. It lasted 120 years, until the ledge beneath it began to crumble away. The citizens of Plymouth, England paid to preserve the lighthouse by dismantling and reassembling it in the town.

The fourth and largest Eddystone Light was built in 1882 on a different rock. Sir James Douglass followed Smeaton's design very closely, and the tower is still standing today. He was the first to use a quick drying cement, which soon became a favorite lighthouse building material.

Corbiere Lighthouse
Jersey, Channel Islands
England

THE SEA HATH NO KING BUT GOD ALONE.

DG Rossetti, *The White Ship*

Boston Light, America's first lighthouse, was built in 1716 on Little Brewster Island near Boston. During the Revolutionary War, the British occupied the light, and American troops twice set it afire. The British repaired it both times only to blow it up when they were finally driven out of the harbor for good. Boston was without light for seven years, until the tower was rebuilt in 1783.

Boston Light
Little Brewster, Boston, Massachusetts
USA

The **Sandy Hook Lighthouse** *was built in 1764 on a narrow sandy strip of land near the New Jersey Shore. It is the oldest original lighthouse still in service in the United States.*

George Washington, first President of the United States, made lighthouse building a national priority. Many lighthouses along the Atlantic coast were built during his term.

In 1789, at President Washington's urging, the United States Congress passed a "Lighthouse Bill"—the ninth piece of legislation enacted by the new government. The bill put all existing lighthouses under federal jurisdiction. Portland Head Lighthouse (1791) off the rugged coast of Maine and Montauk Light (1797) at the tip of Long Island were two of the first lighthouses built during George Washington's presidency.

Portland Head Light
Cape Elizabeth, Maine
USA

Cape Hatteras Light, America's tallest lighthouse at 208 feet, was built in 1789 to guide ships through the "Graveyard of the Atlantic." The first known wreck in these deadly waters off the North Carolina coast occurred in 1526, and since then more than 2000 ships have been lost.

Cape Hatteras Light
Buxton, North Carolina
USA

The lighthouse lifts its massive masonry,

a pillar of fire by night, of cloud by day.

The Lighthouse, 1850
Henry Wadsworth Longfellow (1807–1882)
American poet

23

Built in 1851, Point Amour Lighthouse, *Canada's second highest beacon, marks the northern entrance to the ice-filled Straits of Belle Isle. In 1922, the H.M.S. Raleigh, a British North American Squadron flagship, went aground nearby in dense fog. The remains of the battleship are still visible along the shore below the lighthouse.*

MINOTS LEDGE WAS THE FIRST LIGHTHOUSE BUILT FAR OUT AT SEA—EIGHT MILES EAST OF BOSTON, MASSACHUSETTS—IN THE UNITED STATES. AN IRON SKELETON SEVENTY-FIVE-FEET HIGH, THE LIGHT SWAYED TERRIBLY DURING STORMS, CAUSING MANY KEEPERS TO ABRUPTLY QUIT THEIR POST. IN 1851, IT WAS WASHED AWAY IN A STORM, ALONG WITH TWO ASSISTANT KEEPERS WHO HAD REMAINED ON BOARD.

Phare d'Ar-Men
Brittany
France

When the United States acquired the Alaskan Territory in 1867, there was only one, Russian-built lighthouse in the entire Arctic region. The United States chose not to maintain this light, and it wasn't until 1902 that Congress allowed funds to go to the building of lighthouses in Alaskan waters.

Rockwell Lighthouse
Sitka, Alaska
USA

Statue of Liberty
Liberty Island, New York
USA

EVEN THOUGH SHE CAN'T BE FOUND IN THE COAST GUARD'S LIST OF LIGHTS, THE STATUE OF LIBERTY HAS BECOME THE MOST FAMOUS BEACON OF THEM ALL. SHINING 304 FEET ABOVE ONE OF THE BUSIEST PORTS IN THE WORLD, SHE HAS GUIDED MILLIONS OF IMMIGRANTS TO AMERICA'S SHORES.

The Japanese began building a system of lighthouses along their shores in 1868. Today Japan boasts more than 3,000 navigational markers.

The **Macquarie Light**,

Australia's first lighthouse, was built in 1881 at South Head in the Sydney Harbor.

In the late 1800s Australian engineers developed a successful technique for their environment, a prefabricated hardwood frame clad with iron plates imported from Britain. Many of these early lighthouses are still in use today.

Lighthouse
Notsuke Bay, Hokkaido Island
Japan

Tillamook Lighthouse on the Oregon coast is one of the loneliest and most dangerous towers. It stands on a rock which juts two hundred feet straight up from the ocean floor. Building the tower in 1881 was dangerous work because pounding waves often kept workers from getting on shore.

The Coney Island Light was built in 1890 to guide New York City garbage barges to watery dumps in the Atlantic. The light is still in operation today.

Tillamook Light
Seaside, Oregon
USA

When the **Point Arena Light** was destroyed in the fire that erupted after San Francisco's Great Earthquake of 1906, it was rebuilt with reinforced concrete, a new technique that became the standard for lighthouse construction in America.

Hawaii's most powerful light, **Makaualua Point**, was constructed in 1909. Builders were at first reluctant because the lighthouse was near a leper colony which had been established in 1860 on Molokai Island.

Point Arena Lighthouse
Point Arena, California
USA

BEACONS OF LIGHT AND SOUND

Lead, kindly Light, amid the encircling gloom,

Lead Thou me on!

The night is dark, and I am far from home—

Lead Thou me on!

Light in the Darkness, 1833
John Henry Newman (1801–1890)

Peggy's Cove Lighthouse
Peggy's Cove, Nova Scotia
Canada

In the earliest days, lighthouses used many candles burning together to produce light. Today, the unit of measure for light in a lighthouse is still called "candlepower." One candlepower equals the amount of light made by a single candle.

Candles were the easiest to take care of, but they did not burn very brightly. People began to experiment with fuels such as whale oil and kerosene. The oil was burned in a pan or a lantern with a wick.

Morro Castle Lighthouse
Havana
Cuba

IF A LIGHT IS ONE HUNDRED FEET ABOVE SEA LEVEL, IT CAN
BE SEEN FROM A DISTANCE OF ABOUT THIRTEEN MILES.

Trinidad Memorial Lighthouse
Trinidad, California
USA

Mark Abbott Memorial Lighthouse
Santa Cruz, California
USA

AT THE FOOT OF A LIGHTHOUSE ONE FINDS DARKNESS.

Spanish proverb

In 1782, a Swiss scientist named Aime Argand revolutionized lighthouse technology by inventing a lamp which produced a steady, smokeless, and very bright flame. In Argand's lamp one wick was equal to seven candlepower. The Argand lamp became the standard for more than one hundred years.

At about the same time Argand was inventing his lamp, people were experimenting with shiny metal reflectors. The reflectors were curved bowls placed behind a lamp in order to intensify and bend its light rays.

Punta Celerain Faro
Parque Punta Sur, Cozumel
Mexico

WITH IMPROVED LAMPS AND REFLECTORS, THE STRENGTH OF ONE WICK ROSE TO MORE THAN ONE THOUSAND CANDLEPOWER. PEOPLE SOON FOUND THAT MANY LAMPS WORKING TOGETHER COULD CREATE A LIGHT WITH THE STRENGTH OF SEVERAL THOUSAND CANDLEPOWER.

As technology developed, it was found that rotating a beam allowed the light to be seen from all directions. This resulted in the now familiar revolving lighthouse beam, a development which initially took some getting used to for many mariners.

North Head Light
Cape Disappointment State Park, near Ilwaco, Washington
USA

In 1828, Frenchman Augustin-Jean Fresnel invented the most efficient lens ever used in lighthouses. Experimenting with a drop of honey over a small hole cut out of cardboard, Fresnel discovered a way to magnify light rays into a single powerful beam.

Before Fresnel's invention, the best lamp—which was actually several lamps put together—could produce a light of about 20,000 candlepower. With Fresnel's lens, it increased to 80,000 candlepower. With the introduction of electric power, Fresnel's lens intensified one light to more than a million candlepower. Keepers were required to cover the lantern windows during the day. Otherwise the powerful Fresnel lenses could magnify the sun's rays and start a fire in the lighthouse.

Heceta Head Light
Near Florence, Oregon
USA

Over the years, mariners had trouble distinguishing one lighthouse from another. A system was developed so that each light had its own flashing signal. Each lighthouse was also painted a unique, identifying color. Sailors still carry a list to help them keep track of lighthouses.

Even the most powerful light on earth cannot cut through heavy rain or snow or fog. That is why people realized long ago that sound is a necessary feature of lighthouses. Over the years there have been all kinds of warning sounds used in lighthouses: cannons, gongs, trumpets, bells, whistles, and finally, the fog horn. In 1855, a fog cannon was installed at Point Bonita Light, near San Francisco. The keeper was required to shoot the cannon every half hour when the fog was in, which was nearly all the time. After three days and nights of firing the cannon with only two hours sleep, Sergeant Pat Maloney quit.

Point Bonita Light
Near Sausalito, California
USA

One keeper of the **Wood Island Light** off the Maine coast knew how to deal with his fog warning duties. A dog named Sailor was trained to ring the fog bell by pulling the cord attached to the clapper with its teeth. People used to come from all over to hear Sailor ring the bell.

It was a foghorn from the *Cape Ann Light* *on Thacher's Island, Massachusetts that saved the life of President Woodrow Wilson by preventing the wreck of his fog-blind ship as it returned from Europe in 1919 following the Versailles Peace Conference that officially ended World War I.*

Rock Harbor Light
Middle Island Passage, Lake Superior, Isle Royale National Park, Michigan
USA

West Quoddy Head Light
Lubec, Maine
USA

When a fog bell was installed in the West Quoddy Head Light off the coast of Maine in the 1800s, the keeper asked the government for a raise. Year after year he repeated his request to no avail. Finally, after seven years, his pay was increased $60 a year.

LIGHTHOUSE KEEPERS

W*atchman, what of the night?*

Isaiah XXI. II

Lighthouse keepers
Unidentified location

Throughout history, men, women, and even children have all served as lighthouse keepers, helping to make the coasts safe for mariners. In the days before electricity, keepers had to carry fuel to the top of the light every few hours. This usually meant climbing more than one hundred steps, several times a night. Other duties included making sure the lanterns functioned properly and constantly keeping the lenses and windows at the top of the lighthouse spotless.

Phare de Goury
Pointe de la Hague, Normandy
France

Keepers had a reputation for being fearless in the face of danger. They were often required to rush out into the stormy night in a small boat to attempt daring rescues of shipwrecked sailors.

IT IS UNPLEASANT TO GO ALONE, EVEN TO BE DROWNED.

Russian proverb

Le Phare du Four
Brittany
France

Tibbets Point Light
Cape Vincent, New York
USA

Kate Walker, keeper at Robbins Reef Light in New York from 1894–1919, was only four feet, ten inches, but she performed the tasks of someone twice her size. Like all keepers, she tended the light all night long, seven days a week. Each day she rowed her two small children back and forth to school on the mainland. And she alone rescued many sailors from a watery grave.

During the late 1800s, Idawalley Zorada Lewis, known as Ida, became the most famous lighthouse keeper of her day. In her thirty-nine years as keeper of Lime Rock Lighthouse near Newport, Rhode Island, Ida saved a record number of lives. Many visitors came to the island to meet her, including President Ulysses S. Grant. In 1924 Lime Rock Lighthouse was officially renamed Ida Lewis Lighthouse, the only such honor ever bestowed on a keeper.

In the late 1860s the keeper of the

Hendricks Head Light

in Boothbay Harbor, Maine, pulled an ice-encrusted mattress from the waves after a winter storm. Inside he found a crying baby and a note from the captain of a sinking schooner, committing his darling daughter into God's hands. The keeper and his wife adopted the orphaned girl.

Anythin' for a quiet life, as the man said wen he took the sitivation at the lighthouse.

Pickwick Papers
Charles Dickens (1836-1837)
English writer

Yaquina Head Light
Newport, Oregon
USA

Although they lived an isolated life, keepers usually had
families to share in the lighthouse duties.
Up there among the clouds, my father and the other
keepers have to watch night after night, through storms as
well as pleasant weather, through summer and winter, the
year round, from sunset to sunrise; so that the poor sailors
may be warned off from danger.

Annie Bell Hobbs, 14-year-old daughter of Boon Island Light keeper, circa 1876

Great Duck Island, a lonely piece of land off the

Maine Coast, once boasted a population of eighteen. The keeper of the
light, Nathan Reed, and his wife, Emma, had sixteen children—a
record number for one family living in one lighthouse. A schoolhouse
had to be built on the island for the Reed children. The teacher was the
oldest daughter, who had graduated from school on the mainland.

Pemaquid Point Light
Bristol, Maine
USA

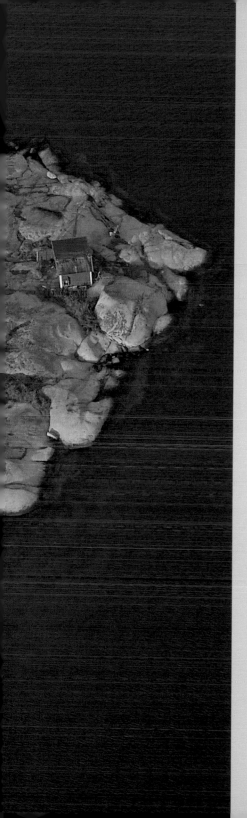

A Maiden gentle, yet, at duty's call,

Firm and unflinching, at the Lighthouse reared

On the Island-rock, her lonely dwelling place.

Grace Darling
William Wordsworth (1770–1850)
English poet

Lighthouse, Hunnebostrand
Bohuslän
Sweden

In the winter of 1856, Sam Burgess—keeper of the twin towers at **Matinicus Light**, twenty-two miles off the coast of Maine—left his post to get supplies and could not return for four weeks due to bad weather. His young daughter, Abby, took care of her invalid mother and three small children, and she kept both lights burning all during the terrible gale. Abby later married a lighthouse keeper and continued to tend lights until the day she died.

As the tide came, the sea rose higher and higher, till the only endurable places were the light towers. If they stood, we were saved, otherwise our fate was all too certain. But for some reason, I know not why, I had no misgivings, and went on with my work as usual.

Abby Burgess, 17 years old, in a letter to a friend describing the time her father was away.

Phare d'Ar-Men
Brittany
France

At the Concord Point Light *in Harre de Grace, Maryland, every keeper was a members of the same family. As a reward for being a hero in the War of 1812, John O'Neil was made keeper of the light. The post passed down to each generation of O'Neils until the light was automated in the 1920s.*

The history books are filled with tragic stories of keepers losing their lives in windswept seas. In 1718, George Worthylake, Boston Light's first keeper, was returning to his post with his wife when a sudden storm swept his rowboat away. A thirteen-year-old Ben Franklin, who was apprenticing with a printer at the time, wrote a ballad about the tragedy. The ballad sold on the Boston streets for a penny.

Grand Haven South Pierhead Light
Grand River, Lake Michigan, Michigan
USA

The lighthouse won't stand over the night.
She shakes two feet each way now.

(This note written by Joseph Wilson—an assistant keeper at Minots Ledge—was found in a bottle several days after the lighthouse was swept away in a hurricane. It was his last.)

Henry Hall was ninety-four years old when he swallowed a piece of molten lead during the fire and ensuing explosion that destroyed the second Eddystone Light in England. Alive but delirious when rescuers arrived, no one believed his story. Henry died twelve days later, and an autopsy revealed a large chunk of metal in his stomach.

KEEPERS WERE KNOWN AS "WICKIES" IN THE DAYS WHEN THEY
TENDED OIL-BURNING LAMPS WITH WICKS.

Mrs. Samuel Bray spent her 1865 Christmas Eve tending the twin towers of Cape Ann Lights on Thacher's Island off the Massachusetts Coast. Her husband, Samuel Bray, a Civil War veteran, had gone to take the ailing assistant keeper ashore for medical attention. A strong wind blew up, and Bray was unable to return until Christmas morning. Mrs. Bray kept both lights burning, going back and forth between the lighthouses, across a quarter-mile stretch of snow and ice and pounding wind.

Hannah Thomas tended **Gurnet Point Light** *in Plymouth, Massachusetts while her husband was away fighting the war of Independence.*

Heceta Head Light
Near Florence, Oregon
USA

In 1789, President Washington visited the

Portsmouth Harbor Light

in New Hampshire. He found its upkeep unsatis-

factory and so he promptly fired the keeper.

Over the years, lighthouses have either closed or become completely automated. Very few lighthouses around the world maintain permanent keepers. The Coast Guard is now responsible for rescue operations at sea.

Marshall Point Light
Port Clyde, Maine
USA

GHOSTS,

PIRATES, PRISONERS, AND CONVICTS

Assistant keepers Joseph Wilson and Joseph Antoine were killed when the Minots Ledge lighthouse was washed away in a hurricane. Ever since the tragedy, local fisherman swear that before a storm a figure can be seen on the ladder which leads from the sea to the lighthouse. The ghostly figure calls out a warning: "Keep away!"

Pemaquid Point Light
Bristol, Maine
USA

Visitors to the Cape Neddick Light off the coast of Maine say they can see the ghostly likenesses of people— perhaps sailors shipwrecked on the shores of the island long ago—in the strange rock formations along the cliffs.

The New London Ledge Lighthouse, built in 1909, supposedly has a resident ghost—a former keeper who was forsaken by his wife and jumped to his death from the tower.

Cape Neddick Light
York, Maine
USA

Saint Simons Island Lighthouse
Off of the Georgia coast, Georgia
USA

The Saint Simons Island Lighthouse off the Georgia coast is said to be haunted by a former keeper killed more than a century ago in a duel with his assistant. Legend has it that he walks the tower steps at night.

The site of Beavertail Light at the entrance to the
Newport, Rhode Island Harbor was used in the 1600s as a hideout
for the notorious pirate, Captain William Kidd. The captain was
eventually caught by the British and hanged in Boston.

Ocracoke Light stands on the island where British
colonial forces captured and killed the notorious pirate Blackbeard
early in the 18th century.

Lighthouse interior
Glasgow
Scotland

Garden Key Light in the Gulf of Mexico was attached to Fort Jefferson, which served as a prison for many years. Its most famous prisoner was Dr. Samuel Mudd who had the misfortune of setting the leg of John Wilkes Booth, President Lincoln's assassin.

CALIFORNIA'S FIRST BEACON, ALCATRAZ LIGHT, WAS CONSTRUCTED IN 1854 NEXT TO A FORT THE SPANIARDS HAD BUILT AND CALLED "THE ROCK." THE FORT WAS LATER TRANSFORMED INTO A MAXIMUM SECURITY PRISON— SUPPOSEDLY A PLACE FROM WHICH NO ONE COULD ESCAPE.

Alcatraz Light
San Francisco Bay, California
USA

Cape Byron Lighthouse
Byron Bay, New South Wales
Australia

Many of Australia's early lighthouses were built by convict labor, including **The Macquarie**, the first lighthouse built in New South Wales. The lighthouse was designed by Francis Greenway, a famous convict architect. Governor Macquarie was so pleased when the lighthouse was completed, he granted Greenway his freedom.

Not everyone was a fan of lighthouses. In the early 1800s in Cape Cod, bands of men known as "Moon Cussers," took advantage of wrecked ships, stealing precious cargo as a means of livelihood. For years, these Moon Cussers, who were sometimes prominent members of the community, fought any attempt to build lighthouses on their shores. But eventually, beacons were built along the coast.

THE COASTWISE LIGHTS OF ENGLAND WATCH THE SHIPS OF ENGLAND GO.

Rudyard Kipling, *The Coastwise Lights*, 1893

In England in the early 17th century, Sir John Killigrew, a known smuggler and privateer, was given a charter by the government to build and operate a lighthouse at **Lizard Point** off the Cornish coast. For years, Killegrew and his "keepers" were responsible for wrecking ships on the treacherous reef and stealing cargo.

Trevose Head Lighthouse
Cornwall
England

Oh dream of joy, is this indeed
The lighthouse top I see?
Is this the hill? is this the kirk?
Is this mine own countree?

The Ancient Mariner
Samuel Coleridge (1772–1834)
English poet

Nugget Point Light
Catlins, South Island
New Zealand